THE Tsunami

OF 1946 AND 1960 AND THE DEVASTATION OF HILO TOWN

By Walt Dudley and Scott C. S. Stone

The Donning Company Publisher
184 Business Park Drive, Suite 206
Virginia Beach, VA 23462

Steve Mull, General Manager
Barbara A. Bolton, Project Director
Pam Forrester, Project Research Coordinator
Dawn V. Kofroth, Assistant General Manager
Sally Clarke Davis, Editor
Betsy Bobbitt, Graphic Designer
Scott Rule, Senior Marketing Coordinator
Patricia Peterson, Marketing Assistant

Library of Congress Cataloging-in-Publication Data
Available upon request

Printed in the United States of America

A wall of water comes ashore on the Big Island of Hawai'i. Mistakenly called "tidal waves," such waves are generated by the displacement of earth, sometimes thousands of miles away, and have nothing to do with tides.

These men race for higher ground, running up Ponahawai Street in Hilo
to get out of the wave-endangered low-lying areas.

Background: When the waves strike they can inundate an area thousands of feet inland;
people ashore are advised to take to higher ground or go two miles inland. The big waves can inspire fear.

Death from the North

1946

BEFORE IT REACHED HAWAI'I that Monday morning the tsunami had already killed.

In the early hours of April 1, 1946, a monstrous wave swept over the lighthouse at Scotch Cape on Unimak Island in Alaska, a concrete structure nearly one hundred feet tall and manned by a crew of five Coast Guardsmen. The last message from the lighthouse reported that an earthquake lasting almost a minute had done no damage. But forty-eight minutes later a wave higher than the lighthouse washed away the big lighthouse, and all its crew.

The earthquake that spawned the great wave took place ninety miles away and under the sea, as the ocean floor began to move. The severity of the earthquake was recorded by sensitive instruments all over the world, but none knew immediately that it took less than an hour to send a 115-foot wave over the lighthouse, nor that the wave was spreading across the Pacific like giant ripples from a rock thrown in a pond, and at an unimaginable scale and speed.

Seismographs at Hawai'ian Volcano Observatory at Kīlauea, on the Island of Hawai'i, and on the University of Hawai'i campus at Mānoa in Honolulu on O'ahu had recorded the quake, but perhaps no one envisioned the devastation that would take place when the waves struck home.

Hawai'i was more than twenty-three hundred miles away from the epicenter, the place of origin, of the earthquake and source of the tsunami, but the waves raced at between 400 and 500 miles an hour and struck the Islands in less than five hours. The "shadow" of water was seen by the crew of a Navy PBY patrol plane, as the waves spread across the Pacific. The crew called their base at Kāne'ohe on the windward side of O'ahu to report "something on the surface of the sea" and was told to drop lower and amplify the report. The aircraft's pilot called back and told the startled radioman at the base that the phenomenon had outrun his plane.

The tsunami reached Hawai'i's northernmost Island of Kaua'i at 5:55 a.m. on that fateful Monday, and moved on to reach Honolulu on O'ahu just thirty-five minutes later.

It would slam into the Island of Hawaiʻi just before 7 a.m., and cause the most casualties and the heaviest destruction of any place in the Pacific.

Tsunami waves roared down the coast of California. At Half Moon Bay the waves carried small boats a quarter of a mile inland, threw an automobile into the front of a house, and drowned an elderly man who had been walking with a friend along the beach in a Santa Cruz cove, while his friend miraculously escaped. Seventeen hours after the beginning of the tsunami it had the strength to swamp fishing boats along the shore of Chile, almost nine thousand miles away. In the Marquesas Islands, waves poured ashore as high as thirty feet.

Hawaiʻi was to suffer the most.

On Kauaʻi, waves came ashore and flowed on five hundred feet inland east of Haʻena. Two women, one holding a baby, became stranded but bravely swam to safety. Others on the Garden Isle were not so lucky, and seventeen people died in the waves.

Creating debris and damage, a wave rushes toward a solitary figure unable to escape. The stevedore (in circle) was swept into the sea and perished.

On Oʻahu, the highest wave reached thirty-six feet at Makapuʻu Point on the Island's south coast, and around this most populous of all the Hawaiʻian Islands, the death toll was six.

On Maui, named for the famous Hawaiʻian demi-god, homes were smashed and vehicles destroyed. The highest waves reached thirty-five feet; fourteen lives were lost, ten of them in a tiny village called Hāmoa, south of Hāna on Maui's east coast.

The tsunami struck the Island of Hawaiʻi, locally called the Big Island —larger than all of the other Hawaiʻian Islands combined—at a time when most people were up and about. An hour earlier and many would still be sleeping when the waves began to hit. It was also the hour before downtown stores would be filled with shoppers. More lives could have been lost, but it was small consolation, for the resultant deaths and damage were staggering.

Continued on page 10

Laupāhoehoe Point, not only low-lying but flat, suffered twenty-four killed in the fierce tsunami; sixteen of the dead were school children.

Looking to the sea down Kalakaua Avenue, a scene of wreckage and abandoned cars. This photo was taken from an area that is now home to the Pacific Tsunami Museum.

Just north of Hilo on the Hāmākua Coast, the small village of Laupāhoehoe was waking to a typical Monday. Some noticed water rising over the seawall—and kept rising. Two waves came in, then a third, larger than the others. They covered the ballfield, swirled around children who had gone down to look at the fish flopping on the shoreline where water had receded, swept around the tennis courts near the shoreline of the low-lying peninsula. Water smashed the grand-stand of the ballpark, where some children had run for safety.

One tenth grader was washed out to sea and deposited on a reef. Another wave arrived and in desperation he dived under it, but one pants leg caught on the reef and he was battered by the water. When his head cleared he found he was floating in debris—and in the company of sharks. A section of flooring from a demolished cottage floated by and he pulled himself up on it, and survived.

Fleeing children noticed the waters seemed to be coming from all sides; others remembered it as "boiling." One man seized two children and ran for safety but was overwhelmed by water, and only by letting one child go could he save the other. People fleeing saw homes and cottages afloat and spinning in the onrushing water. The water became a jumble of trees, branches, boards from houses. A boathouse was demolished. Some children caught by the wild water were saved from being washed out to sea by getting caught in the bushes. Others were taken out to sea and never seen again.

Some of the young teachers, who had come to Laupāhoehoe only a few months earlier and lived in cottages near the water, were swept into the ocean, floated for a while, and disappeared in spite of hastily-organized rescue efforts. Two who could not swim died at once, but another teacher, dragged down twice, was able to hold onto a passing log and survived until a rescue plane could drop her a raft. That afternoon one stunned teacher went back into the ruins of her cottage and brought out only two items: a panty girdle and her college diploma.

In Laupāhoehoe, a village of neighbors, twenty-four people were killed, sixteen of them school children and four of them teachers, the other four being residents.

Between Laupāhoehoe and the town of Hilo lay the Island's largest sugar mill at Hakalau, just fifteen miles north of Hilo. It was also only ten feet above sea level, and the smashing waves ripped into it with a ferocity that virtually destroyed the mill as the waves rose to a height of twenty feet. Along the coast the railroad bridges, built at huge expense because of the necessity of crossing gulches, were destroyed or damaged and at Kolekole Stream, eleven miles above Hilo, an entire portion of a high railroad trestle was twisted off base and carried five hundred feet upstream. In Hilo itself, the railroad station was destroyed and the loss of trestles and trade forced the closure of the railroad company.

On the other side of Hilo proper was Waiākea town, where Hilo had begun to expand by building a railway terminus in 1899. By 1946 the area was prosperous and growing. When the water raced into the area some people climbed on the bridge over the Wailoa River, and when the wave receded, not all were still there. Inside a home in Waiākea an elderly man was reluctant to leave his plants and was washed away by the tsunami, only to turn up safe on the bank of the river. Another man stood near the shoreline with his camera when a wave crashed into the breakwater, throwing boulders the size of automobiles into the air; the photographer decided it was time to seek safety. With his family he drove away, and as he left he saw his neighbor's house being carried toward the sea, bumping into his home as it went.

A home in an unaccustomed place dropped by the tsunami on top of a bridge at the mouth of the Wailoa River.

The boulders thrown up came from the breakwater in Hilo harbor, a breakwater built because the railroad interests lobbied Congress, promising to extend the railway all the way up the Hāmākua Coast. Ships would then be safe in harbor, and could haul sugar from the upland sugar plantations after the sugar was brought to the terminus in Hilo. Congress acquiesced, and construction began in 1908 and was completed in segments, with the last portion completed in 1929. Rocks for the mile-long breakwater came from various places around the Island—Waiākea, Kapoho, Ōlaʻa, Waipiʻo. These were some of the boulders that the tsunami hurled back, some of them weighing more than eight tons, scattered along the beachfront. Sixty percent of the breakwater was destroyed. Beside the boulders on the shore lay massive chunks of coral reef ripped from the ocean and hurled as much as fifteen feet above the normal level of the sea.

As luck would have it, there was only one ship in the harbor that morning, the S.S. *Brigham Victory*. The captain was ashore. In the hold of the ship was fifty tons of dynamite with its blasting caps, and on deck a load of lumber with its lashing removed for unloading—a dangerous situation. The first mate got the ship in motion in just seven

Hilo's piers suffered heavy damage and outright destruction from waves that hammered the shoreline.

minutes, heading past the breakwater for the open sea, and along the way picking up a man whose truck had been washed into the bay, plus a few other survivors. As they sailed to safety, they saw with horror a stevedore on the dock, about to be engulfed by a giant wave. There was no way to save him.

Another stevedore on the docks waiting to unload the ship scrambled inside a warehouse and up in the rafters; he saw that a barge had been flung through one wall and out the other, and bags of sugar were floating beneath him. When he thought it was safe he climbed down again, swam out to the *Brigham Victory*, then about forty feet from the dock, and clambered aboard just as another wave swept away the gangplank. He

looked back at the warehouse in time to see it flattened by the wave. The stevedore became a minister.

Hardest hit by the tsunami was the Hilo bayfront and the strip north of the Wailoa River, the latter now a State park. In 1946 the area north of the river was a largely Japanese settlement known as Shinmachi, Japanese for "new town." It was a close-knit community, its homes built on low-lying ground and close together. Survivors of the wave recall that the strongest building in the area was the Coca-Cola building, and those that could get to it were spared when the second wave struck. The survivors owe their lives to the fact that the bottling plant's manager came to work early that day, so the doors were open.

Outside the building, the homes of Shinmachi were demolished, many of them simply carried away. In Wailoa River, jammed with debris, people were swirling in the swift water, trying to escape and at the same time trying to avoid being struck by floating furniture, parts of buildings, and a myriad of other things torn from the smashed homes. An

enormous wall of water had torn across Shinmachi, killing and devastating.

The bayfront area, generally considered the focal point of the town, became a long stretch of rubble. The stores and shops on the seaward side of Kamehameha Avenue were either turned to splinters or pushed across the street to jam into buildings on the opposite side. The street became impassable, the railway terminus flattened. A lumber yard was torn apart, with lumber being widely scattered. The area took on the look of a village in wartime, battered by artillery. Small boats were flung inland and crushed. Commercial piers were heavily damaged. Water flowed through the streets of the town and people fled ever upward trying to escape the surging water.

For many there was no escape nor any protection for their homes and businesses. Almost five hundred homes or businesses were destroyed in that single day and another one thousand damaged severely. The cost of destruction caused by the killer waves reached an estimated $26 million in 1946 dollars. Far worse was the cost in human lives.

**Even inside buildings, the devastation was complete.
Hilo was forced to undergo a massive rebuilding effort after the tsunami.**

In addition to the 24 dead at Laupāhoehoe, 96 others in and around Hilo lost their lives to the thunderous waves. All around Hawai'i that day, 159 people died in the terror and force of the crushing waves. Only 115 bodies were recovered. In a macabre scene in Hilo, many bodies were taken to an icehouse for storage, and later the bodies were discovered to have frozen together. Before they could be buried they had to be chipped apart with ice picks.

On the north-northeast coast of the Island of Hawai'i the water reached an awesome fifty-five feet in Pololū Valley, while on the southwestern shoreline the height ranged from two feet to as high as twenty feet. Waves charging into Hilo varied from seventeen to twenty-five feet. In places the withdrawal of the water before a wave struck was five hundred feet from the shore; here and there the giant waves from the Aleutians reached more than a half-mile inland.

A few drunks who fished bottles of liquor from the spreading waves found sand inside the bottles; the power of the waves compressed the corks and forced sand inside. The drunks strained the contents through socks and carried on.

For the people of Hilo the tsunami seemed never to end. A total of nine waves came ashore, the first one little more than a fluctuation of water, but the rest was a series of crashing waves that seemed somehow malevolent, cruel cliffs of water that showed no mercy and struck again and again on a town that earlier had seemed so languorous and quiet.

When it was over the hardy people of Hilo began digging out of the rubble, burying their dead and setting out to restructure their shattered lives. Some may have given thought to future tsunamis, but most simply got on with the business of living.

In the wake of the tsunami, Hilo underwent changes. The land between Kamehameha Avenue and the bayfront was converted into a recreation and parking area, with the concept that it would be a buffer zone between the town and future tsunamis. Some of the residential communities were rebuilt, but with wooden homes that were not planned to resist any future waves, and in areas that became crowded. Businesses that had been destroyed were rebuilt, but often in low-lying zones still vulnerable to future tsunami.

And, like the repetition of a bad dream, the tsunami came back.

An earthquake off the coast of Kamchatka sent a tsunami roaring across the Pacific, that hit Hilo at 1:30 p.m. on November 5, 1952, sweeping over small Coconut Island in Hilo Bay, destroying a boat landing down by the piers, destroying a house, swamping the recreational area of Reed's Bay with eleven feet of water, and carrying a fishing sampan two hundred feet inland. The water flooded roads, knocked down telephone poles, and killed six cows. No human lives were lost, and damage totaled less than $800,000.

In 1957 another tsunami generated near the Aleutian Trench hit Kaua'i, where the sea rose more than thirty-two feet, wiped out twenty-five of the twenty-nine homes in one town, and went on to virtually destroy two other small towns. The wave surged into lovely Hanalei Bay. More than seventy-five homes on the Island were destroyed.

The wave moved on to O'ahu, to a height of twenty-three feet, destroying fifty small boats and a half-dozen yachts, damaging docks, engulfing beachfront homes at Lā'ie, and then moved on to Maui and Moloka'i. On Moloka'i the rushing waters ruined a taro crop and smashed a water pipeline at Kalaupapa, the site of the Hansen's Disease community. On Maui the tsunami caused a tremendous vortex in the port of Kahului.

Then Hilo was hit. The waves inundated Coconut Island, snapped the chain of a boat and threw the boat against a bridge, destroying the vessel. Other boats were washed ashore, evoking memories of the destruction of 1946. Structures along the bayfront were damaged, but Hilo was largely spared the devastation of previous tsunami, with no loss of life and damages totaling only $150,000. Throughout the State, the damage reached $5 million.

Continued on page 20

Top: Most of the frame buildings in Waiākea near Hilo were heavily damaged to the point where those on the seaward side of the main street were razed and rebuilt.

Right: The main street of Hilo after the 1946 wave resembled a war zone.

Often Hilo's streets looked as if a giant hand had simply shoved everything out in the open.

The relatively low damage and the lives saved were credited to the Pacific Tsunami Warning System (PTWS) which had alerted police and military authorities, which in turn issued warnings to all who had need to know. Broadcast warning went out not only via official circles, but by commercial broadcast stations.

Scientists, meanwhile, had accumulated new knowledge about tsunamis, with the awareness that each tsunami is unique. Factors that shape the tsunami include the direction of the tsunami in relation to the Hawai'ian Ridge (undersea mountains), bays, and reefs.

But earthquakes do not always generate tsunamis, and the warning system often erred on the side of caution given the speed of the tsunami and the time required to get people alerted and rescue operations put in motion. By 1960 the South Pacific was still without sufficient tide stations to provide data, and in Hawai'i many people became blasé about warnings and came to regard them as false alarms.

Then, out of the sea, a malevolent and remorseless force, the big waves returned.

It was the easiest way to get around Hilo, as these men discovered, and the boat encountered little traffic in the hours following the tsunami.

This "bridge to nowhere" was a major railway bridge before portions of it were swept away by the power of the tsunami. It was later replaced by a highway bridge.

An unintended interaction: this railroad car smashed into the Hatada Bakery in Hilo shows the fury of the tsunami as it swept across the edge of the land.

Railway bridges across the many gulches of the Hāmākua Road were built at great expense, but destroyed in a moment by the tsunami. Here the unsupported rails sag in the aftermath of the devastation.

Buildings lurching up against each other was a common sight after the tsunami.

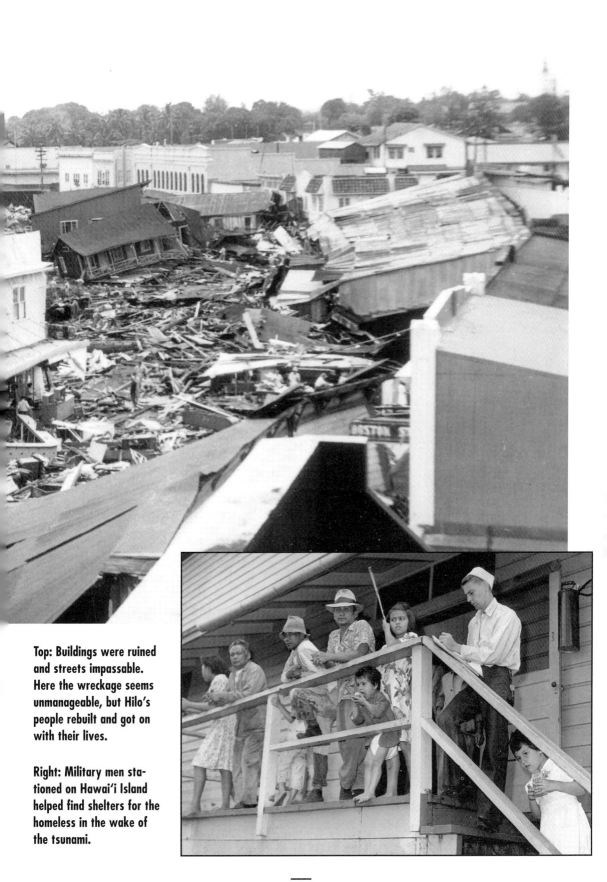

Top: Buildings were ruined and streets impassable. Here the wreckage seems unmanageable, but Hilo's people rebuilt and got on with their lives.

Right: Military men stationed on Hawai'i Island helped find shelters for the homeless in the wake of the tsunami.

Causes of a Tsunami

TSUNAMIS ARE NOT TIDAL WAVES. The destructive mass of water that can reduce a shoreline to splinters has nothing to do with the tides.

Tides are caused by the actions of the sun and moon on the ocean. Tsunamis are caused by the violent movement of land on the shoreline or sea floor, which can occur in any of three ways:

Submarine earthquakes—when a portion of the ocean floor is thrust up or suddenly drops or even thrown sideways, it displaces a massive amount of water. This can happen when the earth's tectonic plates collide, most often in the great ocean trenches. Sometimes the force beneath the plates build up until there is a single massive earthquake, and enough water is set in motion to produce a tsunami.

Landslides—slopes of mountains above or below the sea can become steep with deposits of material that succumb to the pull of gravity. As the deposit of materials increases, the mountain slope becomes more unstable, and a slide can be set off by storms, earthquakes, rain, or just the addition of new material. With a landslide that displaces enough water, a tsunami can occur.

Volcanic activity—the Pacific Rim is perhaps the most geologically active portion of the earth, with its mountains, deep sea trenches, and enough volcanic action to earn it the nickname of "the ring of fire." An eruption in the sea can force into motion large masses of water; similarly, a collapse of the summit of an underwater volcano can generate a tsunami. The buildup of a volcanic mountain in the sea can also result in landslides from the mountain's steep slope.

In all cases, it is the displacement of water that produces the deadly waves.

Boulders, some weighing tons, were tossed from harbor's breakwater onto the streets of Hilo where they were strewn like pebbles.

The Language of Tsunami

TSUNAMI (a word pronounced "soo-nah-mee") is the Japanese term for "great wave in harbor," which the Japanese have experienced often enough.

In Hawai'i the term is "kai e'e," meaning the tsunami waves. Another Hawaiian reference is "kai mimiki," signifying the withdrawal of water before the onrushing "kai e'e."

In France the term is "raz de maree," and in Germany the "flutwellen," and in South America "marimoto."

The scientific community has its own tsunami language.

"Seiche" is a term used to describe another phenomenon when a tsunami strikes. Water in any basin tends to slosh back and forth for a time dependent on the size and shape of the basin. If a tsunami wave hits during the next natural oscillation of the seiche, it can produce an even larger wave than would have been from the tsunami alone. Much of the height of the tsunami waves in bays and harbors is explained by the combination of tsunami wave and seiche. Hawai'ians call the seiche "kai ku piki'o."

"Inundation" is the horizontal distance the waves rush inland from the normal shoreline. "Runup" is the maximum reported wave height on land.

Right: On the coastline north of Hilo, the Hakalau sugar mill functioned as the largest mill on the Island, but with its low-lying locale, was extremely vulnerable to the tsunami in 1946.

Bottom: In the wake of the tsunami, the Hakalau mill and its environment suffered extreme damage.

Piers and rail lines suffered extensively in East Hawai'i, as if the tsunami were bent on destroying transportation.

Many a merchandising plan died in the debris of Hilo.

Top: Interior scenes easily matched scenes of destruction outside. This business establishment in Kona, on the leeward side of the Island, proved few places were safe from the tsunami's fury.

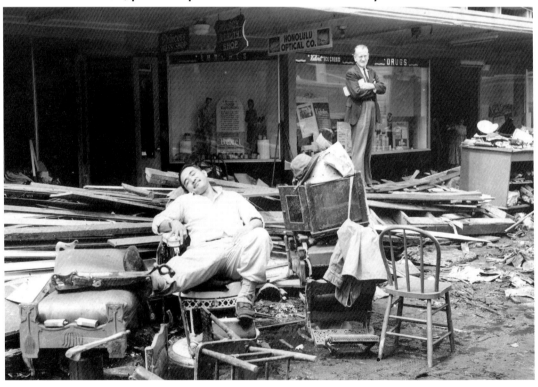

A tired worker takes a break from cleaning up Hilo. T. V. Lum Ho was among many who worked long, difficult hours to restore some semblance of order to the town.

Top: On the Kona coast, the force of the tsunami smashed into fishing boats along a long stretch of coastline.

This U.S. Army crash boat was hurled from its usual environment deep inland, and heavily damaged.

Life goes on—but not until the debris is cleaned up and people can get a grip again on their lives.

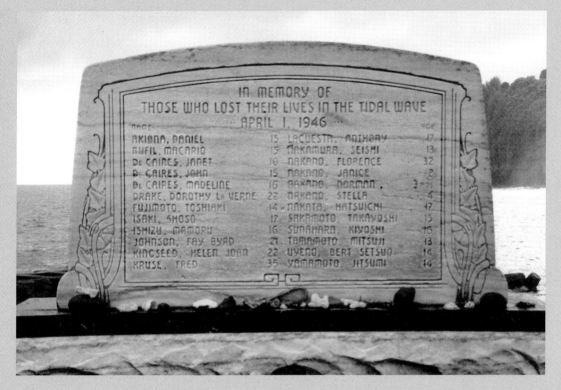

After the 1946 tsunami this memorial was erected a Laupāhoehoe Point in memory of the victims; there were twenty-four names inscribed.

Past Deadly Tsunami in Hawai'i

Date	Source	Locations in areas with casualties	Casualties	Runup (in feet)
1837	Chile	Hilo, Hawai'i	14	20
		Kahului, Maui	2	20?
1868	Hawai'i	Ka'ū, Hawai'i,	46	60
		Puna, Hawai'i	1	20
1877	Chile	Hilo, Hawai'i	5	16
1923	Kamchatka, Russia	Hilo, Hawai'i	1	20
1946	Aleutians	Hawai'i, Maui,	159	55 (maximum)
		O'ahu, Kaua'i		
1960	Chile	Hilo, Hawai'i	61	35
1975	Hawai'i	Halapē, Hawai'i	2	26

The Hilo Theatre stands amid the wasteland left by the tsunami, but was so damaged inside it had to be demolished.

Background: A wall of water comes ashore on the Big Island of Hawai'i.
Mistakenly called "tidal waves," such waves are generated by the
displacement of the earth, sometimes thousands of miles away,
and have nothing to do with tides.

Death in the Night

1960

THE EARTHQUAKE TOOK PLACE AT CONCEPTION, in Chile, a town that lay between the Andes Mounains and the great Peru-Chile Trench. Two more earthquakes followed, devastating the narrow southern coast. Waves swept over homes and ships, strips of land sank, and buildings were washed out to sea. Two thousand people died, and damages were $417 million.

And that was not the end of it.

The tsunami hit Easter Island, destroying a temple on which the Islanders had built some of the massive and famous statues, carrying some of them nearly five hundred feet away. In Honolulu, officials of the Tsunami Warning Center issued a tsunami warning.

It was 6:47 p.m. on May 22, 1960.

At 8:30 p.m. coastal sirens in Hilo began to sound. Shortly after 9 p.m., radio stations carried reports from Tahiti that the waves were only three feet high. (Few realized that most of French Polynesia was relatively safe from tsunami because of well-developed reefs, which tend to minimize a tsunami's effects.) A report from Tahiti at 10:23 p.m. was the first official confirmation other than reports from Chile, that indicated a tsunami had taken place.

Just before 11 p.m. the tsunami reached Samoa, causing no loss of life and only some $50,000 in damage. But Pitcairn Island, New Guinea, New Zealand, the Philippines, and Okinawa all were hit by the tsunami, and some three hundred lives were lost. Damage was recorded in Oregon, California (forty boats were sunk and two hundred damaged in Los Angeles), and on the Kamchatka Peninsula. Astonishingly, the tsunami reached Japan a full twenty-four hours after the Chilean earthquakes, ten thousand miles away. The waves took 140 lives and caused more than $50 million in damage along the Japanese coast.

On the Island of Hawai'i, reports about the small wave at Tahiti fueled the feeling of many residents that the tsunami report was another false alarm. A change in the Civil Defense sirens also caused confusion as people waited for a second siren that never

In a scene Hilo residents hoped never to see again, the tsunami of 1960 left its mark. These parking meters all point seaward, evidence of the tsunami's power as it receded.

sounded. All of Hilo waited for the estimated time of arrival of midnight for the tsunami, and many of the curious went down to the shore to see what was happening. Just after the new day arrived, May 23, water rose four feet above normal, then fell to three feet below normal.

A radio station reported that no waves had arrived and the arrival time set back a half-hour. The report proved that communications between the media and the warning system had broken down. At 12:46 a.m., a second crest washed under the bridge across the Wailoa River, which had been the scene of so much disruption in the 1946 tsunami. Water began to withdraw again and at 1 a.m. was seven feet below normal.

Geologists described what happened next: ". . . the sound, a dull rumble like a distant train that came from the darkness far out toward the mouth of the bay . . . a pale wall of tumbling water, the broken crest of the third wave, was caught in the dim light thrown across the water by the lights of Hilo . . . at l:04 a.m., the 20-foot-high nearly vertical front of the in-rushing bore churned past . . . brilliant blue-white electrical flashes from the north end of Kamehameha Avenue a few hundred yards south of where we waited signaled that the wave had crossed the sea wall and buffer zone and was washing into town with crushing force. Flashes from electrical short circuits marked the impact of the wave as it moved swiftly southeastward along Kamehameha Avenue.

The Wailoa Bridge shattered by the waves. In the background is a power plant, damaged but intact.

Dull grating sounds from buildings ground together by the waves and sharp reports from snapped–off power poles emerged from the flooded city now left in darkness behind the destroying wave front. At 1:05 a.m. the wave reached the Hawaiʻian Electric (HELCO) power plant at the south end of the bay, and after a brief greenish arc that lit up the sky above the plant, Hilo and most of the Island of Hawaiʻi was plunged into darkness."

Despite warnings that included pleas from the governor, people waited in the night along the shoreline to see what the tsunami might bring, and for many it brought death. Once again, the highest casualty toll, sixty-one, and the heaviest damage, an estimated $50 million, took place in Hilo. Damage to property included 229 homes and 508 businesses. Floodwaters inundated approximately 580 acres between the Wailuku River and the breakwater's shoreward end. Between the two rivers, Wailuku and Wailoa, the water washed inland as far as the twenty-foot contour above sea level.

Nowhere else in Hawaiʻi was there a loss of life. Hilo not only suffered casualties and damage, but was paralyzed in the aftermath. Water mains were broken, sewage systems destroyed, and public shelters had to house 215 families for a time.

Over the city lay a pall of devastation. Parking meters were bent parallel to the ground and facing the sea, reminders of the wave's force and danger from debris even in withdrawal. Buildings were leveled along Kamehameha Avenue once again. Bulldozers had to be brought in to push the rubble aside. The homes and buildings of Waiākea and Shinmachi once again were smashed as they were in 1946.

Medical professionals worked around the clock, and discovered some new hazards. People rescued from polluted flood waters developed infections that sometimes took months to clear up, and physicians afterwards would talk about the necessity of keeping ample antibiotics on hand.

As the four destructive waves hit Hilo (and there were other, smaller waves), the big waves tore twenty-two-ton boulders from the ten-foot high seawall and carried them as far as six hundred feet inland. The reinforced Hilo Iron Works building, right down in the path of the waves, survived the force of the wave but its second-story skylights were blown away by air pressure as the waves struck. The large, modern hardware store, Hawai'i Planing Mill, was swept away in a thirty-five-foot wave and pieces of it were found fifteen hundred feet away. Some city blocks were leveled. Buildings constructed of light-weight materials often simply floated out to sea. Trucks and autos were wrecked, sometimes stacked three deep by the waves.

Lengths of curb from the bayfront highway, some as long as 30 feet, were torn up and carried 350 feet inland. Once more the footbridge to Coconut Island, rebuilt and strengthened after the tsunami of 1946, 1952, and 1957, was torn away. Fishing boats were thrown ashore and overturned, and most of the fleet that had not put out to sea was wiped out.

The first two waves of the tsunami were relatively harmless, lulling people into a false sense of security so that they returned to danger areas —and were crushed by the remorse-less power of the third wave. These unnecessary deaths raised questions: The Hawai'i National Guard—which was activated after the tsunami to keep order and prevent loot-ing— might have been activated in advance to keep people out of the danger areas. The warning system worked as it was designed to work, but the public in general was vague about how the warning was presented, and how they were expected to respond. Now, before them, lay a city stricken twice in the past fourteen years, with friends and rel-atives and neighbors dead or hurt or homeless, and it was obvious that something must be done.

Like some strange, abstract modern sculpture, these autos exhibit the destructive power of the giant waves from the sea.

Women search the fields for items of property flung from their homes by the waves.

Eight days after the tsunami's terror, the Hawai'i Redevelopment Agency was established to put Hilo back together again. In time the buffer zone on the ocean side was extended and a landfill plateau constructed raising the inland border of the greenbelt by twenty-six feet—and incidentally creating a pleasant and attractive bayfront area of green grass and open spaces. Federal and State funds for public housing were made available and the Small Business Administration (SBA) provided the funds to get businesses in business again. The local populace might be forgiven if the citizens were hesitant about building again, even behind the buffer zone. In a show of confidence, state and county buildings were built first, on a bluff overlooking the buffer zone.

Continued on page 50

Learning from the tsunami, Hilo's Civil Defense officials plan for the next one, among other things, by establishing evacuation routes out of the town.

Empty shoes tell their own story, but of a victim or of a survivor?

Bottom: For many, the cleanup and rebuilding effort seemed overwhelming, but it got done all the same, giving Hilo residents a deserved reputation for fortitude.

A family salvages what they can of their battered home.

Right: A clock in the rubble of Hilo's bayfront notes the early-morning time of the destructive tsunami. The clock was salvaged to be turned into a monument. (Top) Today the clock stands as a monument and as a reminder.

The 1960 tsunami's strike in the early morning darkness added to the confusion and terror.

The morning after seemed, to many Hilo residents, like a terrible dream.

Scientists have concluded that each tsunami is unique. The two major tsunamis of 1946 and 1960 were as different as they were deadly. The 1946 tsunami brought waves of fifty-five feet with an average of thirty feet along the northeast coast. These heights were more than twice the heights of the waves around the rest of the Island. In the 1960 tsunami the Island's shore facing the direction of Chile, the epicenter of the earthquakes, might have been expected to show a similar pattern—higher on that shore, smaller elsewhere on the Island—but waves were no higher than on the other, protected coasts. Additionally, the flooding pattern from the two tsunami was different in Hilo. One conclusion became apparent—tsunamis originating in different geographic locales tend to cause different patterns of flooding in Hawai'i.

Not all tsunamis are born far from the Island's shore.

On April 2, 1868, a major earthquake hit Hawai'i Island, cracking the earth of Puna and Ka'ū like an eggshell. It caused a huge landslide in Wood Valley in Ka'ū covering a distance of 2.5 miles and burying alive thirty-one people and more than five hundred horses, cattle, and goats. It generated a tsunami that swept homes off the shore at Keauhou Landing. Nine years later a tsunami was generated southwest of Kona on the leeward coast; in 1908 an earthquake struck again, probably accompanied by a landslide, and a volcanic landslide in 1919 caused a runup of fourteen feet in the area of Ho'ōpū-loa. Earthquakes and landslides in 1951 and 1952 originated in Kona and Kalapana, the latter now largely covered in lava from an eruption that began in 1953. In 1975 a 7.2 earthquake struck the Island of Hawai'i. Boy Scouts and accompanying adults were camping at Halape, only fifteen miles from the epicenter of the earthquake. The campers ran toward the ocean to escape a rockslide from a nearby mountain, only to be faced with a tsunami. Two of the campers were killed and nineteen injured. Four of the ten horses on

This surrealistic sculpture is a car wrapped around a tree by the unimaginable force of the tsunami.

51

Autos seemed particularly susceptible to being deposited by the waves in places where they didn't belong.

the shore were killed. Damage was widespread all over the Island, and totaled more than $4 million. A total of eight houses, three businesses and twenty-seven fishing boats were destroyed or suffered extensive damage. The land along the shore dropped by more than eleven feet and moved south twenty-six feet—and all from a tsunami that originated locally.

Whether the origins are near or far, the tsunami will come again, and Hilo Bay has proved to be the most vulnerable area of the Islands. The area faces directly toward the Aleutians, which spawned the tsunami of 1946 and 1957. Even without a direct line-of-sight positioning, Hilo has suffered from tsunamis that sweep around the Island and reach their maximum height—and power—in Hilo.

Since written records began in the early nineteenth century, at least a dozen tsunamis have roared onto the shore in Hawai'i killing 291 people, more than earthquakes, volcanic eruptions, and hurricanes together. Nothing has changed that would mitigate the awesome movement of land beneath or alongside the sea, or soften the impact of great waves born in the land's upheaval. The waves will come again as surely as the displacement of land will continue, and the waves will move across the Pacific at incredible speeds, sometimes with little or no warning, to crash onto the shore with unimaginable power.

Outwitting the Wave

IF A TSUNAMI APPEARS IMMINENT, it's likely you will know about it, via Civil Defense warning sirens, via the Emergency Alert Systems which uses all local radio stations to warn listeners, or even via word of mouth from other people. If none of these take place and you are in a remote area and feel an earthquake, get to high ground immediately.

If you are a visitor, be aware that a tsunami watch is called about once a year, but few are upgraded to warning status. Still, tsunamis are a fact of life in Hawai'i, with the Islands being hit by a tsunami on the average of every seven years since records have been kept. If you feel an earthquake, go immediately to at least one hundred feet above sea level or two miles inland. If this is impossible, get to the third floor or higher of a reinforced concrete building (going inland and higher is safer). Wait for authorities to inform you that the danger is over.

If you are a resident, you should understand the importance of obeying Civil Defense rules. You must remember the history of tsunamis in the Islands and stay away from the seashore. If you are aware of a sudden rise or fall of the ocean, move to high ground immediately and do not return until authorities inform you the danger has passed. Consider keeping a "tsunami kit" in your home, consisting of water, battery-operated radio and a first aid kit, leaving room for your valuables which can be collected. When you go higher and inland, stay there until you are notified by authorities that the danger has passed.

You do not have to be a tsunami victim, if you take proper precautions.

Water and debris in the streets meant an extensive cleanup and a planned restoration that eliminated all building on the seaward side of Kamehameha Avenue, the main street of Hilo.

The Pacific Tsunami Museum

PROBABLY QUITE A FEW PEOPLE thought there should be a tsunami museum to help with tsunami education, but it was articulated forcefully by Jeanne Johnson, who survived the 1946 tsunami, and years later suggested a museum be established.

In Hawai'i in the past seventy-five years, ten tsunamis have caused 223 deaths and approximately $60 million in reported property damage. The tsunami of 1946 was the worst natural disaster ever to occur in Hawai'i, with Hilo alone reporting 96 of the 159 deaths in the State, and more than $26 million in 1946 dollars in damage.

In 1994 the Pacific Tsunami Museum was incorporated as a non-profit organization with the mission of providing educational programs for people of Hawai'i and Asia/Pacific. Ironically, the planned organizational meeting of the board of the proposed museum on October 4, 1994, had to be postponed because of a tsunami alert. It did take place later, and the Museum became a reality. The Museum received a boost when First Hawaiian Bank donated the C. W. Dickey Building, a 1930 structure at 130 Kamehameha Avenue in downtown Hilo, to be a permanent home for the Museum. The donation took place on May 22, 1997, and the building has since been renovated and remodeled to become an attractive and functional museum.

Since its inception the Museum has become an authoritative voice on tsunami matters in the State of Hawai'i, and has provided numerous educational programs and projects.

Surfing the Wave
Gambling with Death

IN MOST IF NOT ALL OF TSUNAMI WARNINGS, surfers race down to their favorite surfing areas and await the Ultimate Wave. It is even more foolish than playing Russian Roulette, for the crushing power of the waves make it long odds that any surfer will survive.

Only one man is known to have surfed a tsunami, and he did not have a choice. In 1868 a local tsunami killed forty-six people and caused extensive damage, and also gave birth to a surfing legend as reported at the time by a Mr. C. C. Bennett. Bennett wrote:

"I have just been told of an incident that occurred at Ninole, during the inundation of that place. At the time of the shock on Thursday, a man named Holoua, and his wife, ran out of the house and started for the hills above, but remembering the money he had in the house, the man left his wife and returned to bring it away. Just as he entered the house the sea broke on the shore, and enveloping the building; first washing it several yards inland, and then, as the wave receded, swept it off to sea, with him in it. Being a powerful man, and one of the most expert swimmers in that region, he succeeded in wrenching off a board or a rafter, and with this as a papa hee nalu (surfboard) he boldly struck out for the shore, and landed safely with the return wave. When we consider the prodigious height of the breaker on which he rode to shore (fifty perhaps sixty feet), the feat seems almost incredible, were it not that he is now alive to attest it, as well as the people on the hill side who saw him."

Holoua was lucky. No surfer today can expect that kind of luck.

The Japanese Language School in Waiākea was picked up by the waves
and left astride automobiles in the tsunami flotsam.

A Hilo Gas Company tank amazingly survived, but not the houses washed
into the Waiolama canal near downtown Hilo.

Buddhist officials gather following the 1960 tsunami to hold a memorial service for the dead.

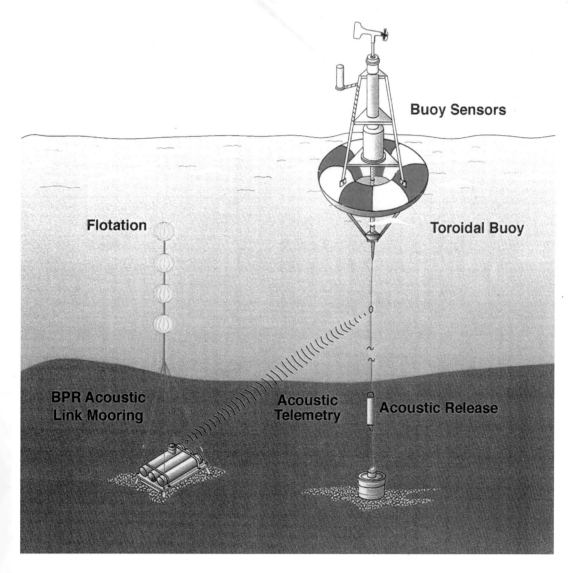

Satellite

Tsunami Data Telemetry

Buoy Sensors

Flotation

Toroidal Buoy

BPR Acoustic
Link Mooring

Acoustic
Telemetry

Acoustic Release

Design of the tsunami real-time reporting system using deep-water tsunami detectors. This new system should help improve the reliability of the tsunami warning system.

Facing page: Deployment of a surface buoy for a deep-water, real-time tsunami detector being operated by NOAA's Pacific Marine Environmental Laboratory.

The Warning System

By 1948 AN OFFICIAL SYSTEM was established to warn potential targets of a tsunami. The system is called Pacific Tsunami Warning System (PTWS) and has its headquarters at Ewa Beach on the Island of O'ahu. It is the center of a network of twenty-six member nations in the Pacific and operates thirty tidal stations. In addition it can request data from another one hundred such stations operated and maintained by the National Ocean Service. The PTWS can receive seismic data from hundreds of seismic stations around the world through the National Earthquake Information Center in Golden, Colorado. The PTWS coordinates activities of regional tsunami warning centers in Alaska, French Polynesia, Chile, Japan, and Russia.

Most of the tsunamis generated in the Pacific result from geologic changes taking place on the ocean floor and generating an earthquake of 7 or more on the Richter scale. The activity is picked up within minutes on seismograph stations around the world, and its epicenter, or exact location, is pinpointed. Within a half-hour the PTWS has identified the location and magnitude of the earthquake, and issues a "tsunami warning" for those areas that could be hit in three hours or less. This still doesn't allow enough time to confirm the existence of the tsunami waves and allow for evacuations, so evacuation procedures are undertaken immediately. A "tsunami watch" is issued for the remainder of the Pacific.

The first indication of a tsunami wave usually comes from the tidal station nearest the disturbance, when waves appear on a station tide gauge, larger than a normal recording. Sea level gauges can be monitored by the PTWS, and if nothing abnormal has been recorded, the warning and watch are canceled. But if indications are that a tsunami has been generated, the watch is upgraded to a warning.

In Hawaii, reports of a potential tsunami alert the police departments, Civil Defense, the American Red Cross and others. Local broadcast media may air the "tsunami watch." There is a general awareness on the part of the public. If the situation warrants a "tsunami warning," then the Hawaii State Emergency Broadcast System begins broadcasting it on all commercial radio stations and Civil Defense officials begin ordering evacuation of low coastal areas that may be endangered. Sirens sound, and the Islands are on alert.

A great advantage of the PTWS system is that it can predict the arrival time of the first tsunami waves. This is possible by using a formula that includes the depth of the water it is passing through. Since the depth of most ocean basins have been determined, oceanographers can determine the tsunami wave's speed.

The PTWS uses computers to estimate the arrival time. Ironically, the effectiveness of the system itself caused some problems in the 1950s and 1960s, when the PTWS predicted tsunamis which did occur, but were small and caused the public to believe the predictions were false alarms. In 1952 and 1957, dangerous tsunami struck Hawaii but caused no casualties, thanks to the PTWS.

Today, this is how the warning/alert system is designed to work for the public:

Three hours before the arrival of the first wave the Civil Defense sirens will sound the alert signal—a three-minute steady siren tone. It means, "turn on your radio." Radio stations will switch to the State Emergency Alert System (EAS) and regular announcements will be made concerning the status, procedures to follow, and any updated tsunami information. The siren is sounded again at two hours, one hour and a half-hour before the estimated arrival time of the waves. Each signal is accompanied by EAS announcements. Stay tuned to the announcements to learn of the all-clear. Dangerous waves may continue for several hours.

NOTICE
IN CASE OF TIDALWAVE
RULE 1- STAY CALM
RULE 2- PAY HOTEL BILL
RULE 3- RUN LIKE HELL

One hotel owner along Hilo's Banyan Drive posted a sign that reflected his philosophy of how to behave in the face of the next tsunami.

Acknowledgments

THE STUDY OF TSUNAMI is an ongoing science and much remains to be learned about the characteristics of these powerful, swift and deadly waves. But much good science has been accomplished and there is a heightened awareness of the waves and their origins. One entity given over to the education of the public about tsunami is the Pacific Tsunami Museum in downtown Hilo. Individuals connected with the Museum have become expert, and two of them were helpful in compiling this book.

One is Mrs. Donna Saiki, whose cheerful assistance is much appreciated. Another is Jim Wilson, publisher of the Island's leading newspaper, *The Hawai'i Tribune Herald.* Jim has maintained a long interest in tsunami and was a source of both data and inspiration. Photos in this book came from a variety of sources, but all were provided by the Pacific Tsunami Museum.

In acknowledging good help, we hold all others blameless for any errors that may appear in this book, and assume responsibility for those errors. We hope this book will inform and enlighten visitors and residents alike about the destructiveness of the tsunami, so that the next tsunami will be far less destructive.

And there will be a next one.

The Authors

About the Authors

DR. WALTER C. DUDLEY is Professor of Marine Geology and Oceanography and Director of the Kalakaua Marine Education Center at the University of Hawai'i at Hilo. He is an author with Mrs. Min Lee of the book, *Tsunami!,* and has published more than fifty scientific articles in oceanography, including the marine science entries in the *Cambridge General Encyclopedia.* Dudley has been featured in tsunami documentaries on *National Geographic Explorer,* the Discovery Channel, the History Channel, and the Learning Channel. A former Captain in the paratroopers and a black belt in karate, he lives in Papaikou, Hawai'i, with his wife, Kamila, and four children.

SCOTT C. S. STONE is a former foreign correspondent for international media, including Reuters, the Cox Newspapers and The New York Times News Service, specializing in Asia/Pacific affairs. He has written more than two dozen books including a suspense novel which won an "Edgar" (as in Oscar). He also has written a national prize-winning film script. Pursuing dual careers, Stone also is a retired Navy Commander and a combat veteran of two wars, including duty as an advisory officer to paramilitary forces sailing junks on the rivers and around the coastline of Vietnam. He has maintained a residence in Hawai'i for more than forty years. He and his wife, Walelu, live in Volcano Village.

Photo Credits